这本《唐可儿奇遇记》属于

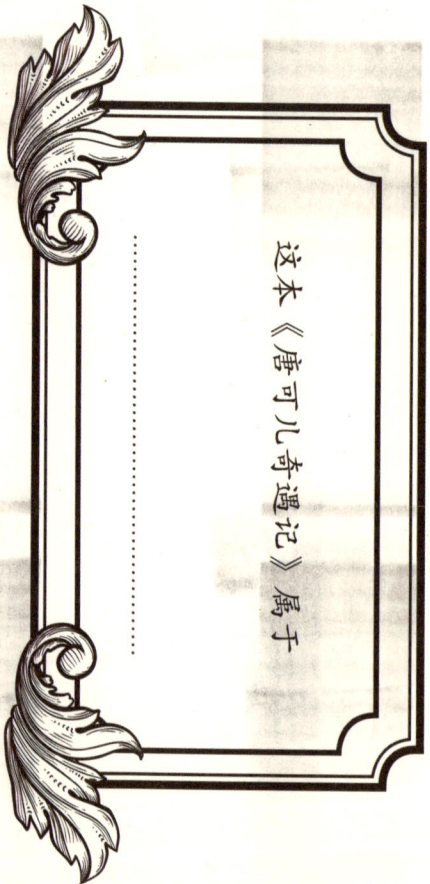

· · · · · · · · · · · · · · · · · ·

唐可儿奇遇记

TWINKLE'S ENCHANTMENT

唐可儿梦游仙境

【美】莱曼·弗兰克·鲍姆 著

【美】梅金尼尔·恩赖特 绘

易晓燕 译　　晓 华 + Emma 朗读

中国国际广播出版社

图书在版编目（CIP）数据

唐可儿梦游仙境：汉英对照/（美）莱曼·弗兰克·鲍姆著；易晓燕译.
北京：中国国际广播出版社，2016.11
（唐可儿奇遇记）
ISBN 978-7-5078-3900-5

Ⅰ.①唐… Ⅱ.①莱…②易… Ⅲ.①英语—儿童读物 Ⅳ.①H319.4

中国版本图书馆CIP数据核字（2016）第241518号

唐可儿奇遇记：唐可儿梦游仙境

著　　者	［美］莱曼·弗兰克·鲍姆
译　　者	易晓燕
责任编辑	李芬芳　李　卉
版式设计	国广设计室
责任校对	徐秀英

出版发行	中国国际广播出版社 ［010-83139469　010-83139489（传真）］
社　　址	北京市西城区天宁寺前街2号北院A座一层
	邮编：100055
网　　址	www.chirp.com.cn
经　　销	新华书店
印　　刷	北京艺堂印刷有限公司

开　　本	650×950　1/16
字　　数	80千字
印　　张	7
版　　次	2016 年 11 月 北京第一版
印　　次	2016 年 11 月 第一次印刷
定　　价	42.00 元（含mp3光盘）

让优秀的双语桥梁书引领孩子进入英语文学世界（代序）

晓华

....

《唐可儿奇遇记》是美国儿童文学家弗兰克·鲍姆（L. Frank Baum）所著的另一隐秘的奇幻佳作，风靡西方百年后，首次在中国面世。作为《绿野仙踪》的作者，鲍姆在中国可算是大名鼎鼎，但知道或读过《唐可儿奇遇记》的人却并不多。

弗兰克·鲍姆是位极为高产的作家。他一生写过六十二本书，大多数都是为孩子写的，其中光是由《绿野仙踪》的故事延伸出来的奥兹国系列小说就有十四本，此外还有不少书，其中的人物多与奥兹国有关。

《唐可儿奇遇记》是一个完全独立的童话故事系列，以生活在草原小镇上的小姑娘唐可儿为主角，讲述了她在动物世界的神奇冒险。与《绿野仙踪》中的多萝西一样，唐可儿活泼大胆、心直口快，并且，据说这两个人物的原型，其实是同一个人，都是鲍姆妻子的外甥女玛格达雷娜。玛格达雷娜一家住在达科他草原的埃奇利小镇上，鲍姆笔下的唐可儿也住在埃奇利小镇。而多萝西的家乡虽然在堪萨斯，可《绿野仙踪》中描写的她家周围的环境，与达科他草原其实并无二致。

　　有意思的是，在《唐可儿奇遇记》首次出版时，鲍姆并没有署自己的名字，而是使用了笔名 Laura Bancroft。鲍姆的大量作品都使用了不同的笔名，有人说这是因为他太能写了，用笔名是不想市面上同时出现太多部他写的书，互相之间形成竞争。不过，也许是因为这套小说出版之后卖得太好，又或许是鲍姆认为这一系列和《绿野仙踪》一样都是自己的得意之作，到《唐可儿奇遇记》再版的时候，他就又署回了本名，弗兰克·鲍姆。

《唐可儿奇遇记》系列包括六本小说，此次中国国际广播出版社带给读者的是其中的三本。《唐可儿梦游仙境》主要讲述了唐可儿去大峡谷采蓝莓，她不听甲壳虫的警告，越过了那条魔法线，遇到了能说会动的石头；喜欢吃奶油的蝴蝶；跑得飞快的书本以及故弄玄虚的黄鼠狼等奇妙的现象，并受邀参加舞会的故事。《糖块山》中的故事，则是在潜移默化中帮助孩子了解社会层次，两个孩子无意中进入神秘的城市，在其中遇上各色人群，应付审问和意外，还见证假冒的贵族如何身份败露以及焦虑的公主如何保住地位。《解救泥龟王子》的故事梗概是，唐可儿在小溪边玩耍时抓住了一只会说话的泥龟，经过一番冒险之后，帮助它变回了仙境王子。

　　《唐可儿奇遇记》中的故事传达出的，是人和动物间相互尊重、和谐相处的讯息。比如，在《土拨鼠先生》中，鲍姆借着土拨鼠先生之口，说出了这样一段话："你们残忍地对待可怜的动物，而他们不过是别无他法，找不到吃的就得饿死。其实广阔的田野上生长的东西足够人类和我们都吃的。"

在鲍姆看来，人类按照自己的利益划分动物好坏，进而铲除"坏动物"的行为，实在是一种残忍。

青蛙吃蚊子，所以需要保护；蝗虫吃庄稼，于是需要消灭。在大人们的世界里，按照自己的利益来划分动物是有益还是有害并没有什么不妥。可孩子们不一定这样看。他们对自然世界的尊重，似乎已经超越了我们。前几天，我和女儿Emma在小区散步时，发现一只长尾长身的鼠族动物在马路上一蹿而过。我心里一阵硌硬，正想把过街老鼠的成语解释给她听，她却嚷道："啊！好可爱的大老鼠！"说得我无言以对。也许，像《唐可儿奇遇记》这样以自然和动物为题材的童话故事，之所以受到孩子们的喜爱，正是因为这些故事跳出了一般大人们那狭隘的善恶观吧。

《唐可儿奇遇记》系列是鲍姆专为年龄较小的读者写的章节书，文字上比《绿野仙踪》更简单，也更短小精悍，适合八岁以上、英语水平较好的孩子独立阅读。从亲子阅读到独立阅读，是一个了不起的跨越，也是养成阅读兴趣和习惯的关键期。孩子从依偎在父母身边聆听、翻看绘本，到独自探索英文文字的世界，这期间，寻找到合适的阅读内容对他们至关重要。专门为大孩子而写的章节书，可以说是一个完美的过渡。章节书在词汇、句子长度和内容方面都照顾到年轻读者的需求，篇幅比绘本长了许多，插图减少了，但是故事分成了一个个短章节，一天看不完没关系，夹上书签，把书放在枕边，第二天接着看就好了。

我特别遗憾自己在少年时期没能接触到这样的章节书。在原版英文读物并不丰富的年代，我的英文阅读之旅，从《新概念英语》开始，一下就蹦到了《简爱》《荆棘鸟》之类的经典小说。这些大部头不光生词多，深刻程度也超出我的理解范围，导致我不得不跳过大段大段的描写。直到现在我看原版小说还有个坏习惯，就是看不大进去风景描写，一味贪图情节发展。章节书，对于循序渐进的阅读，对于培养良好的阅读习惯，真是太重要了。

《唐可儿奇遇记》系列的英文版每个故事大约四五千字，分为八个章节，也就是说每一章只有七百个字左右，再加上每本书都配有十几张精美的彩页插图，孩子们读起来一定不会觉得累。书的排版上也充分照顾到孩子们，中英双语分段排版，遇到不认识的字词可以迅速查到中文。如果读得累了，还可以听一听我和女儿 Emma 录制的双语朗读版，用耳朵享受大师的经典之作。其实听书，也是一种重要的语言学习方式。不管孩子还是大人，在阅读有一定难度的文字时，是不是都特别希望有人能读给自己听？这是因为，听书时眼睛得到了解放，并且，优美的朗读，可以使人更容易进入到文字描绘出的情境中去。

　　在各类儿童英文读物已经很丰富的当下，为孩子选择经典佳作显得尤为重要。一套好的作品，会引领孩子进入英语文学的殿堂。而好书不会被时间埋没。我相信，弗兰克·鲍姆的这套《唐可儿奇遇记》，一百年后仍然会焕发光彩，受到中国孩子们的喜爱。

目录
List of Chapters

唐可儿
进了大峡谷

Twinkle
Enters the Big Gulch

有一天下午，唐可儿决定进一趟大峡谷，给爸爸的晚饭采点儿蓝莓。她穿上蓝色花布格子连衣裙，戴上蓝色的太阳帽，脚上蹬了一双结实的鞋，提上锡桶就出门了。

妈妈在厨房门口冲着唐可儿喊："及时赶回来吃晚饭哦。"

ONE afternoon Twinkle decided to go into the big gulch and pick some blueberries for papa's supper. She had on her blue gingham dress and her blue sun-bonnet, and there were stout shoes upon her feet. So she took her tin pail and started out.

"Be back in time for supper," called mamma from the kitchen porch.

唐可儿一边蹦蹦跳跳地往门外跑，一边说："当然啦。我现在还不饿，不过，快到晚饭时我肯定会饿坏的。所以我一定会赶回来吃饭的。"

峡谷离唐可儿家没多远，说是峡谷，更像是一个大沟，只是崖壁并不太陡峭，可以爬下去，峡谷中间是逶迤绵延的小山丘和一些深沟，满山遍野都是灌木、藤蔓和一些开花的植物，这些植物在这个地方可不常见。

"'Course," said Twinkle, as she trotted away. "I'm not hungry now, but I'll be hungry 'nough when supper-time comes. 'Course I'll be back!"

The side of the gulch was but a little way from the house. It was like a big ditch, only the sides were not too steep to crawl down; and in the middle of the gulch were rolling hills and deep gullies, all covered with wild bushes and vines and a few flowering plants—very rare in this part of the country.

唐可儿在达科他这个地方住了没多久，因为爸爸在峡谷附近买了个新农场才搬过来的。这个巨大的壕沟带给她无穷的欢乐，她喜欢在里面闲逛，摘一些平原上没有的浆果和花花草草。

　　今天，她小心翼翼地从房子后面的小路边上爬下去，很快就到了谷底。然后她开始寻找莓果。可惜之前来摘过的地方现在连个莓果的影子都找不到了，所以她觉得还是得再走远一点儿。

Twinkle hadn't lived very long in this section of Dakota, for her father had just bought the new farm that lay beside the gulch. So the big ditch was a great delight to her, and she loved to wander through it and pick the berries and flowers that never grew on the plains above.

To-day she crept carefully down the path back of the house and soon reached the bottom of the gulch. Then she began to search for the berries; but all were gone in the places where she had picked them before; so she found she must go further along.

唐可儿进了大峡谷

Twinkle Goes Into the Gulch

她先坐下来歇歇脚，不经意间抬头瞥了一眼对面，一簇灌木丛映入了眼帘，上面挂满了熟透的蓝莓——就在对面崖的半壁上。

她以前从没到过这么远的地方，但她知道要想为爸爸的晚餐采到莓果，就必须要爬上山坡，摘到这些蓝莓。于是她站起身，朝着那个方向走了过去。所有这些对小姑娘来说都是那么新鲜，就像一个迷人的仙境。不过她丝毫没有察觉到峡谷已被施了魔法。

She sat down to rest for a time, and by and by she happened to look up at the other side and saw a big cluster of bushes hanging full of ripe blueberries—just about half way up the opposite bank.

She had never gone so far before, but if she wanted the berries for papa's supper she knew she must climb up the slope and get them; so she rose to her feet and began to walk in that direction. It was all new to the little girl, and seemed to her like a beautiful fairyland; but she had no idea that the gulch was enchanted.

不一会儿，路上爬来一只甲壳虫，唐可儿停下来给它让路，这时她听到甲壳虫说话了：

"小心那道魔法线！再不注意可就要快跨过去了。"

"什么魔法线？"唐可儿问。

"都快到你眼皮底下了。"小东西回答。

Soon a beetle crawled across her path, and as she stopped to let it go by, she heard it say:

"Look out for the line of enchantment! You'll soon cross it, if you don't watch out."

"What line of enchantment?" asked Twinkle.

"It's almost under your nose," replied the little creature.

"可我什么也看不见呀。"她嘀咕着仔细看了又看。

"你当然看不见啦，你知道，魔法线要是人人都能看得见，那可还叫什么魔法线啊，不管是谁，要是跨过去就会看到奇妙的事，来一次不可思议的冒险。"甲壳虫侃侃而谈。

"我才不在乎呢!"唐可儿说。

"I don't see anything at all," she said, after looking closely.

"Of course you don't," said the beetle. "It isn't a mark, you know, that any one can see with their eyes; but it's a line of enchantment, just the same, and whoever steps over it is sure to see strange things and have strange adventures."

"I don't mind that," said Twinkle.

唐可儿遇到了甲壳虫

Twinkle Meets the Beetle

"好吧，你不在意的话，我也不管了。"
甲壳虫说完蠕动着过了小路，钻进一块大石头
下面不见了。

　　唐可儿继续朝前走，一点儿都不害怕。要
是甲壳虫说的是真的，果真有一条看不见的线
把真实的世界和被施了魔法的世界隔开的话，
那她倒有点儿等不及想赶快跨过去，小女孩们
都会这么想的。

"Well, I don't mind if you don't," returned
the beetle, and by that time he had crept across
the path and disappeared underneath a big rock.

Twinkle went on, without being at all afraid.
If the beetle spoke truly, and there really was
an invisible line that divided the common, real
world from an enchanted country, she was very
eager to cross it, as any little girl might well be.

她一下子想到在遇到甲壳虫之前肯定就已经越过魔法线了，不然她听不懂甲壳虫的话，也不知道他在说什么呀。

And then it occurred to her that she must have crossed the enchanted line before she met the beetle, for otherwise she wouldn't have understood his language, or known what he was talking about.

唐可儿心里很清楚，在真实世界里，孩子才不会和甲壳虫说话呢。她一边反复琢磨，一边不慌不忙地往前走，忽然，有个声音向她大喊：

"小心！"

Children don't talk with beetles in the real world, as Twinkle knew very well, and she was walking along soberly, thinking this over, when suddenly a voice cried out to her:

"Be careful!"

第二章
Chapter II

滚 石
The Rolling Stone

唐可儿立马站住了，她向四周望了望，纳闷是谁在说话呢。看了一圈也没看到一个人。于是，她又开始往前走。

　　"小心点儿啊，不然你就踩到我了！"那个声音再次大喊。

　　唐可儿非常谨慎地看了看她的脚。除了一块又大又圆的石头和一株带刺的蓟外，脚边没有什么别的东西啊，那块石头有她的头那么大。她才不会往带刺的蓟上踩呢。

OF course Twinkle stopped then, and looked around to see who had spoken. But no one was anywhere in sight. So she started on again.

"Look out, or you'll step on me!" cried the voice a second time.

She looked at her feet very carefully. There was nothing near them but a big round stone that was about the size of her head, and a prickly thistle that she never would step on if she could possibly help it.

她问："是谁在说话？"

有个声音在回答："哎哟，是我在说话啊。你觉得会是谁呢？"

"我不知道，"唐可儿说。"我可没看到有什么人。"

"那你也太目中无人啦，"那声音说，"我是滚石，离你的左脚趾也就两英寸远。"

"Who's talking?" she asked.

"Why, *I'm* talking," answered the voice. "Who do you suppose it is?"

"I don't know," said Twinkle. "I just can't see anybody at all."

"Then you must be blind," said the voice. "I'm the Rolling Stone, and I'm about two inches from your left toes."

"滚石！"

"嗯，就是我，我是不生苔藓的滚石。"

"你不可能是滚石。"唐可儿干脆在小路上坐了下来，仔细打量起了这块石头。

"怎么就不是啦？"

"The Rolling Stone!"

"That's it. That's me. I'm the Rolling Stone that gathers no moss."

"You can't be," said Twinkle, sitting down in the path and looking carefully at the stone.

"Why not?"

"因为你没在滚啊。当然，你确实算是一块石头。这我能看得出来，但你没在滚啊。"她说。

"真笨！"石头回答。"我叫滚石就得每分钟都滚来滚去？"

"可不就是那样，"唐可儿回答。"你要是不滚的话，就只是一块普通静止的石头呀。"

"Because you don't roll," she said. "You're a stone, of course; I can see that, all right. But you're not rolling."

"How silly!" replied the Stone. "I don't have to roll every minute to be a Rolling Stone, do I?"

"Of course you do," answered Twinkle. "If you don't roll you're just a common, *still* stone."

唐可儿仔细地打量起了这块石头

Twinkle Looks Carefully at the Stone

"哦，天哪！"石头有点受不了了，"你简直什么都不懂啊。你是一个会说话的姑娘，对吧？"

"可以肯定，我当然是啦。"唐可儿说。

"可你不是每分钟都在说话吧？"

"妈妈说我每分钟都不停地说。"她回答。

"Well, I declare!" exclaimed the Stone; "you don't seem to understand anything. You're a Talking Girl, are you not?"

"To be sure I am," said Twinkle.

"But you don't talk every minute, do you?"

"Mama says I do," she answered.

"但是你不是每分钟都在说。你有时会安静下来，对吧？"

"是啊。"

"我也一样啊。有时我会滚，所以人们叫我滚石。你有时说话，所以你是会说话的姑娘。"

"不，我是唐可儿。"她说。

"But you don't. You're sometimes quiet, aren't you?"

"'Course I am."

"That's the way with me. Sometimes I roll, and so I'm called the Rolling Stone. Sometimes you talk, and so you're the Talking Girl."

"No; I'm Twinkle," she said.

"唐可儿听起来不像是一个名字。"石头说。

"反正爸爸就这么叫我。"小姑娘解释说。然后，想到她已经逗留了太长的时间，她补充说：

"我要上山来采摘一些浆果。既然你会滚，那和我一起去吧。"

"什么！上山？"石头大喊。

"That doesn't sound like a name," remarked the Stone.

"It's what papa calls me, anyway," explained the girl. Then, thinking she had lingered long enough, she added:

"I'm going up the hill to pick those berries. Since you can roll, suppose you go with me."

"What! Up hill?" exclaimed the Stone.

"怎么啦？"唐可儿问。

"谁听说过石头能滚上山？这太不正常啦！"

"任何石头都能滚下山坡，"唐可儿说。"如果你不能滚上山，你和一块普通的鹅卵石没什么两样。"

"哦，如果我非得这么做的话，我可以滚上山。"石头没好气地大声说。

"Why not?" asked Twinkle.

"Who ever heard of a stone rolling up hill? It's unnatural!"

"Any stone can roll down hill," said the child. "If you can't roll up hill, you're no better than a common cobble-stone."

"Oh, I can roll up hill if I have to," declared the Stone, peevishly.

"但是，这是件苦差事，我的背几乎会断的。"

"我看不出你还有背。"唐可儿说。

"哎呀，我浑身都是背。"石头回答说，"当你的背疼的时候，你只是身体的一部分在疼。但是，当我的背酸痛的时候，我除了中间一点之外浑身都会疼。"

"But it's hard work, and nearly breaks my back."

"I can't see that you have any back," said Twinkle.

"Why, I'm all back," replied the Stone. "When *your* back aches, it's only a part of you. But when *my* back aches, it's all of me except the middle."

"中间的疼才是最要命的。"唐可儿一本正经地说着站起了身，又加上一句，"好吧，要是你不想去，那咱们再见吧。"

"友善点儿嘛。"石头说，深深地叹了口气。"我会陪你去啦。但滚下山要比滚上山容易得多，我向你保证！"

"天哪，你太爱发牢骚了！"唐可儿大喊。

"The middle ache is the worst of all," said Twinkle, solemnly. "Well, if you don't want to go," she added, jumping up, "I'll say good-bye."

"Anything to be sociable," said the Stone, sighing deeply. "I'll go along and keep you company. But it's lots easier to roll down than it is to roll up, I assure you!"

"Why, you're a reg'lar grumbler!" exclaimed Twinkle.

"那是因为我过着艰苦的生活，"石头说着，有点儿闷闷不乐。"但是，咱们可别吵起来，我很少有机会与社会上和我立足点相同的人说话。"

"你没有任何的立足点，都没有脚。"唐可儿大声说，向着石头摇了摇头。

"That's because I lead a hard life," returned the Stone, dismally. "But don't let us quarrel; it is so seldom I get a chance to talk with one of my own standing in society."

"You can't have any *standing*, without feet," declared Twinkle, shaking her head at the Stone.

"至少是一个有理解力的人，理解力是一个人拥有的最好的立足点。"甲壳虫还嘴说。

　　"大概是这样吧，"唐可儿说，一副若有所思的表情，"但我还是很高兴我有腿。"

"One can have *understanding*, at least," was the answer; "and understanding is the best standing any person can have."

"Perhaps that is true," said the child, thoughtfully; "but I'm glad I have legs, just the same."

第三章
Chapter III

千奇百怪
的过客

Some Queer
Acquaintances

"等一下！"传来一个细小的声音，唐可儿注意到一只黄色蝴蝶刚刚落到了这块石头上。"你不是从农场来的孩子吗？"

"是呀。"她应声回答，听到蝴蝶说话特别开心。

"那你能告诉我，你妈妈今天会搅奶油吗？"漂亮的小东西边说边缓缓地扇动着纤巧的翅膀。

"WAIT a minute!" implored a small voice, and the girl noticed a yellow butterfly that had just settled down upon the stone. "Aren't you the child from the farm?"

"To be sure," she answered, much amused to hear the butterfly speak.

"Then can you tell me if your mother expects to churn to-day," said the pretty creature, slowly folding and unfolding its dainty wings.

"等一下"

"Wait a Minute"

30

"你问这个干什么？"

"要是她今天搅的话，我就飞到那边的房子里去弄些奶油来。要是不搅东西，我就飞到山谷，打劫我知道的蜂巢。"

"你怎么又抢又偷的？"唐可儿问。

"只有这样我才能活下去啊。"蝴蝶说。

"Why do you want to know?"

"If she churns to-day, I'll fly over to the house and try to steal some butter. But if your mother isn't going to churn, I'll fly down into the gulch and rob a bees' nest I know of."

"Why do you rob and steal?" inquired Twinkle.

"It's the only way I can get my living," said the butterfly.

"从来没有人给我吃的，我只能自己想办法弄到我想吃的。"

"你喜欢奶油？"

"当然啦！要不我们怎么会被叫做蝴蝶呢（译者注：蝴蝶的英文拼写中含有'奶油'一词）。我最喜欢奶油了，听说有些国家的孩子总会在窗台上留一小碟奶油，这样我们什么时候饿了就能随便吃了。真希望我也能生在那样一个国家里啊。"

"Nobody ever gives me anything, and so I have to take what I want."

"Do you like butter?"

"Of course I do! That's why we are called butterflies, you know. I prefer butter to anything else, and I have heard that in some countries the children always leave a little dish of butter on the window-sill, so that we may help ourselves whenever we are hungry. I wish I had been born in such a country."

"妈妈周六前都不会搅奶油的，"唐可儿说。"我知道，因为我得帮她，我不喜欢做奶油！"

"那我今天不去农场了，"蝴蝶回答说，"再见，小姑娘。要是你记得的话，在我够得到的地方留一碟奶油吧。"

"好吧，"唐可儿说。蝴蝶扇动着翅膀，在空中翩翩飞舞，朝着峡谷下面飞去了。

"Mother won't churn until Saturday," said Twinkle. "I know, 'cause I've got to help her, and I just hate butter-making!"

"Then I won't go to the farm to-day," replied the butterfly. "Good-bye, little girl. If you think of it, leave a dish of butter around where I can get at it."

"All right," said Twinkle, and the butterfly waved its wings and fluttered through the air into the gulch below.

这时小姑娘开始上山了，滚石跟在她身边慢慢地滚着，因为地面高低不平而不停地唠叨抱怨着。

不久，她发现一本小书正在横穿小路，这本小书比邮票大不了多少。它的两条腿像大黄蜂的那样又细又长，就是靠着这样两条长腿，它跑得飞快，夹带起的风把树叶扇得疯狂摇摆，书是半打开着的。

Then the girl started up the hill and the Stone rolled slowly beside her, groaning and grumbling because the ground was so rough.

Presently she noticed running across the path a tiny Book, not much bigger than a postage-stamp. It had two slender legs, like those of a bumble-bee, and upon these it ran so fast that all the leaves fluttered wildly, the covers being half open.

"那是什么？"唐可儿吃惊地看着那本书问。

"那是小学究，"石头回答。"提防着点儿它，听说它可是个危险的家伙。"

"它已经没影儿了。"唐可儿说。

"别管它啦，我知道没有人需要它。帮我上一下这个坡，行吗？"

"What's that?" asked Twinkle, looking after the book in surprise.

"That is a little Learning," answered the Stone. "Look out for it, for they say it's a dangerous thing."

"It's gone already," said Twinkle.

"Let it go. Nobody wants it, that I know of. Just help me over this bump, will you?"

小学究

The Little Learning

于是，她帮石头滚上了一个小山坡，这时候，她的注意力被一阵奇怪的噪音吸引住了，"啪！啪！啪！"

"什么东西啊？"唐可儿问，犹豫着要不要继续前进。

"只是一只黄鼠狼。"石头回答。"过不了一分钟，你就会看到他啦。每当他认为四下无人，没人会听到，就会弄出'啪''啪'的声响。"

So she rolled the Stone over the little hillock, and just as she did so her attention was attracted by a curious noise that sounded like "Pop! pop! pop!"

"What's that?" she inquired, hesitating to advance.

"Only a weasel," answered the Stone. "Stand still a minute, and you'll see him. Whenever he thinks he's alone, and there's no one to hear, 'pop' goes the weasel."

果然，一个小动物很快从他们走的那条路穿了过去，每走一步都会发出滑稽的声音。当他发现唐可儿在盯着他看时，就立刻不再弄出这种声音，马上冲进一簇高高的草丛中躲了起来。

现在，他们快到那片浆果树丛了，唐可儿走得特别快，滚石使出浑身的力气才能跟上她。可是当她到浆果树丛的时候，她发现一群奇怪的鸟正在以最快的速度吃那些浆果。

Sure enough, a little animal soon crossed their path, making the funny noise at every step. But as soon as he saw that Twinkle was staring at him he stopped popping and rushed into a bunch of tall grass and hid himself.

And now they were almost at the berry-bushes, and Twinkle trotted so fast that the Rolling Stone had hard work to keep up with her. But when she got to the bushes she found a flock of strange birds sitting upon them and eating up the berries as fast as they could.

那些鸟并不比知更鸟大多少，他们包裹着一层柔软的光滑的肌肤，而不是羽毛。他们的黑眼睛溢满着欢乐，细长的喙，从他们的鼻子下弯曲伸出，这给他们的脸增添了几分俏皮的表情。鸟的身上没有羽毛，这倒没让唐可儿感到奇怪，可每只鸟的尾巴上都有一根超级长的羽毛，着实让唐可儿大吃一惊，这太不可思议了。

The birds were not much bigger than robins, and were covered with a soft, velvety skin instead of with feathers, and they had merry black eyes and long, slender beaks curving downward from their noses, which gave to their faces a saucy expression. The lack of usual feathers might not have surprised Twinkle so much had she not noticed upon the tail of each bird one single, solitary feather of great length, which was certainly a remarkable thing.

一羽鳥

The Birds of One Feather

"我知道他们是什么，"唐可儿说，明白了似的点了点头，"他们是一羽鸟。"

　　听到这么说，这些鸟哄堂大笑，其中一只鸟说："也许你认为那就是我们聚集在一起的原因吧。"

　　"嗯，难道不是这个原因吗？"唐可儿问。

"I know what they are," she said, nodding her head wisely; "they're birds of a feather."

At this the birds burst into a chorus of laughter, and one of them said: "Perhaps you think that's why we flock together."

"Well, isn't that the reason?" she asked.

"和那个一点关系都没有，"那只鸟声明。
"我们聚集在一起的原因是我们很骄傲，不愿
和那些浑身都是羽毛的普通鸟混在一起。"

"我本来想你们会感到羞愧，因为你们看
上去光秃秃的。"唐可儿回答。

另一只鸟啄起一颗蓝莓咽了下去，说道：
"事实上是，唐可儿，在这个世界上普通的东
西没什么了不起的。

"Not a bit of it," declared the bird. "The
reason we flock together is because we're too
proud to mix with common birds, who have
feathers all over them."

"I should think you'd be ashamed, 'cause
you're so naked," she returned.

"The fact is, Twinkle," said another bird, as
he pecked at a blueberry and swallowed it, "the
common things in this world don't amount to much.

地球上有成千上万只鸟，但是只有我们少数几只只有一根羽毛。在我看来，如果你头上只有一根头发，你会更漂亮。"

"我敢肯定我会更'与众不同'。"唐可儿说，用了一个她能想到的最难的词。

There are millions of birds on earth, but only a few of us that have but one feather. In my opinion, if you had but one hair upon your head you'd be much prettier."

"I'd be more 'strord'nary, I'm sure," said Twinkle, using the biggest word she could think of.

"每个人的品味都不一样。"滚石评论道，他费力滚了一路，刚到唐可儿身边。"拿我来说，我既没有头发也没有羽毛，我对此感到很高兴呀。"

　　"There's no accounting for tastes," remarked the Rolling Stone, which had just arrived at Twinkle's side after a hard roll up the path. "For my part, I haven't either hair or feathers, and I'm glad of it."

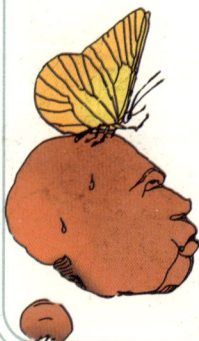

听了这些话，鸟儿们又大笑了起来。他们吃完了喜欢的浆果，飞向了空中，一会儿便没了踪影。

The birds laughed again, at this, and as they had eaten all the berries they cared for, they now flew into the air and disappeared.

第四章
Chapter IV

跳舞熊
The Dancing Bear

"是真的啊，我不知道原来有这么多东西都会说话呢。"唐可儿说，她开始采浆果，把它们放进桶里。

"这是因为你身处被施了魔法的那部分山沟里。"滚石回答，"当你再次回家中的时候，你会觉得所有的一切只是一个梦罢了。"

"REALLY," said Twinkle, as she began picking the berries and putting them into her pail, "I didn't know so many things could talk."

"It's because you are in the part of the gulch that's enchanted," answered the Rolling Stone. "When you get home again, you'll think this is all a dream."

"我想知道这是不是一个梦！"唐可儿突然哭了，她停下来环顾四周，然后仔细体会自己的感受。"这些通常都出现在爸爸读给我的童话故事里。我不记得什么时候入睡的，但没准儿我确实睡着了。"

"别为这事儿烦了。"滚石说，伴随着发出一声怪响，唐可儿想滚石是在笑吧。"如果你醒来，你会难过没做个更长的梦；如果你发现你没有睡着，这将是一次奇妙的探险。"

"I wonder if it isn't!" she suddenly cried, stopping to look around, and then feeling of herself carefully. "It's usually the way in all the fairy stories that papa reads to me. I don't remember going to sleep any time; but perhaps I did, after all."

"Don't let it worry you," said the Stone, making a queer noise that Twinkle thought was meant for a laugh. "If you wake up, you'll be sorry you didn't dream longer; and if you find you haven't been asleep, this will be a wonderful adventure."

"说得再对不过了，"小姑娘回答，并重新开始采摘浆果装进桶里。"我要是告诉妈妈这一切，她一个字都不会信的。而爸爸肯定会笑笑，捏捏我的脸颊，说我像梦游仙境的爱丽丝，或者像在奥兹国的多萝西。"

就在这时，她发现了一大团黑乎乎的东西从对面灌木丛里走出来，当她看清是一头硕大的熊用后腿支撑着站在她身边的时候，她的心怦怦地跳得飞快。

"That's true enough," the girl answered, and again began filling her pail with the berries. "When I tell mama all this, she won't believe a word of it. And papa will laugh and pinch my cheek, and say I'm like Alice in Wonderland, or Dorothy in the Land of Oz."

Just then she noticed something big and black coming around the bushes from the other side, and her heart beat a good deal faster when she saw before her a great bear standing upon his rear legs beside her.

熊的头上戴着一顶红色的小帽子，帽子由一根橡胶松紧带固定着。他长着一双小眼睛，不过圆溜溜的小眼却灼灼有神，因为从他露出的两排洁白的牙齿来看，他似乎是带着一脸的笑容。

"不要害怕，那只是一头跳舞熊。"滚石喊道。

"这个孩子为什么会害怕？"熊问。轻柔的语调让唐可儿想起了小猫的咕噜声。

He had a little red cap on his head that was kept in place by a band of rubber elastic. His eyes were small, but round and sparkling, and there seemed to be a smile upon his face, for his white teeth showed in two long rows.

"Don't be afraid," called out the Rolling Stone; "it's only the Dancing Bear."

"Why should the child be afraid?" asked the bear, speaking in a low, soft tone that reminded her of the purring of a kitten.

"还没有一个人听说过跳舞熊会伤害人的。我们能算得上是世界上最无害的动物了。"

"你真的是一头会跳舞的熊吗？"唐可儿好奇地问。

"是的，亲爱的。"熊回答说，低头鞠了一个躬，然后骄傲地抱着双臂，好像靠在附近的一块大石头上似的。"真希望这儿能有个人可以告诉你我的舞跳得有多好。自夸对我来说太不谦虚了，你知道的。"

"No one ever heard of a Dancing Bear hurting anybody. We're about the most harmless things in the world."

"Are you really a Dancing Bear?" asked Twinkle, curiously.

"I am, my dear," he replied, bowing low and then folding his arms proudly as he leaned against a big rock that was near. "I wish there was some one here who could tell you what a fine dancer I am. It wouldn't be modest for me to praise myself, you know."

唐可儿遇到了跳舞熊

Twinkle Meets the Dancing Bear

"我觉得自夸是不太谦虚，"唐可儿说，"但是如果你真是一头跳舞熊，那你为什么不跳舞呢？"

"又来了！"滚石大喊。"唐可儿这丫头想让每个人都不停地动。起初，她也不相信我是滚石，因为我正静静地躺着。现在，她又不相信你是一头跳舞熊了，因为你没在不停地跳舞。"

"I suppose not," said Twinkle. "But if you're a Dancing Bear, why don't you dance?"

"There it is again!" cried the Rolling Stone. "This girl Twinkle wants to keep every body moving. She wouldn't believe, at first, that I was a Rolling Stone, because I was lying quiet just then. And now she won't believe you're a Dancing Bear, because you don't eternally keep dancing."

"嗯，确实还是有些道理的。确切地说，我在跳舞的时候才能算是一头跳舞熊，而你只有滚动的时候才能算是滚石。"熊表明了自己的观点。

"我不敢苟同你。"滚石冷冰冰地回应道。

"好了，不管怎么说我们别再争论了。"熊说。"我邀请你们两个来我的山洞里看我跳舞。看完我跳舞后，唐可儿肯定会认为我是一头跳舞熊的。"

"Well, there's some sense in that, after all," declared the Bear. "I'm only a Dancing Bear while I'm dancing, to speak the exact truth; and you're only a Rolling Stone while you're rolling."

"I beg to disagree with you," returned the Stone, in a cold voice.

"Well, don't let us quarrel, on any account," said the Bear. "I invite you both to come to my cave and see me dance. Then Twinkle will be sure I'm a Dancing Bear."

唐可儿和熊继续前行

Twinkle and the Bear Continue Their Walk

"我的桶还没满呢。"小姑娘说，"我一定要为爸爸的晚餐采摘到足够的浆果。"

"我来帮你吧。"熊礼貌地说。并且当即开始采摘浆果放到唐可儿的桶里面。他的大爪子看上去又笨拙又别扭，但是熊用它的大爪子采摘下的蓝莓数量却是惊人的。唐可儿要想赶上他太费劲了。在她几乎还没意识到这双大爪子是如何采摘得那么快的时候，小桶已经装满了颗粒饱满的上好浆果。

"I haven't filled my pail yet," said the little girl, "and I've got to get enough berries for papa's supper."

"I'll help you," replied the Bear, politely; and at once he began to pick berries and to put them into Twinkle's pail. His big paws looked very clumsy and awkward, but it was astonishing how many blueberries the bear could pick with them. Twinkle had hard work to keep up with him, and almost before she realized how fast they had worked, the little pail was full and overflowing with fine, plump berries.

"现在，我会带你到我的山洞去。"熊说。

　　他把她的手放到他柔软的爪子里，领着她沿着陡峭的山前行，滚石急急忙忙地在他们身后滚动着。不过他们没走多远，唐可儿的脚下一滑，为了不让自己摔倒，她使劲推了滚石一把，害得他从小径上跌了下去。

"And now," said the Bear, "I will show you the way to my cave."

He took her hand in his soft paw and began leading her along the side of the steep hill, while the Stone rolled busily along just behind them. But they had not gone far before Twinkle's foot slipped, and in trying to save herself from falling she pushed hard against the Stone and tumbled it from the pathway.

石头在往下滚

The Fall of the Rolling Stone

"现在你办到了！"石头大声咆哮，身体同时在猛烈地旋转着。"我这就要开始滚了，因为我失去了平衡，不由自主啦！"

　　就在大石头还在说话的时候，他已经沿着沟的一面飞了下去，在小山丘和岩石上跌跌撞撞——有时会跃到空中，然后又紧贴向地面，但每一分钟都滚得越来越快。

　　"天啊。我担心滚石会受伤的。"唐可儿眼睛盯着滚石说。

"Now you've done it!" growled the Stone, excitedly, as it whirled around. "Here I go, for I've lost my balance and I can't help myself!"

Even as he spoke the big round stone was flying down the side of the gulch, bumping against the hillocks and bits of rock—sometimes leaping into the air and then clinging close to the ground, but going faster and faster every minute.

"Dear me," said Twinkle, looking after it; "I'm afraid the Rolling Stone will get hurt."

"那算不上危险。他和岩石一样坚硬，这沟谷里没一样东西可以伤害他一下的。不过我们的朋友得滚很长时间才能再次回到这里，所以我们别等他了。走吧，亲爱的。"熊回答说。

"No danger of that," replied the Bear. "It's as hard as a rock, and not a thing in the gulch could hurt it a bit. But our friend would have to roll a long time to get back here again, so we won't wait. Come along, my dear."

他再次伸出爪子，唐可儿一只手握住了它，另一只手提着桶，这样，崎岖的山路就不那么难走了。

He held out his paw again, and Twinkle took it with one of her hands while she carried the pail with the other, and so managed to get over the rough ground very easily.

第五章
Chapter V

有瀑布
的山洞
The Cave of the
Waterfall

不久，他们来到了洞口。因为洞口从外面看过去阴暗潮湿，唐可儿把身子缩了回来，并且说她估计是不会进去的。

"但是里面很亮堂，那里还有一条很漂亮的瀑布呢。不要害怕，唐可儿，我会照顾好你的。"熊说。

BEFORE long they came to the entrance to the cave, and as it looked dark and gloomy from without Twinkle drew back and said she guessed she wouldn't go in.

"But it's quite light inside," said the bear, "and there's a pretty waterfall there, too. Don't be afraid, Twinkle; I'll take good care of you."

于是小姑娘鼓起勇气，同意让熊领着她进山洞。很快她就为进到山洞里而不是做一个胆小鬼而感到高兴了。因为这个地方很宽敞，屋顶上有许多裂缝，这让充足的阳光和空气透射进来。四周侧壁有几双大耳朵，似乎是在岩石上雕刻出来的。这些让小姑娘感到大为震惊。

"这些耳朵是干什么用的？"她问。

So the girl plucked up courage and permitted him to lead her into the cave; and then she was glad she had come, instead of being a 'fraid-cat. For the place was big and roomy, and there were many cracks in the roof, that admitted plenty of light and air. Around the side walls were several pairs of big ears, which seemed to have been carved out of the rock. These astonished the little girl.

"What are the ears for?" she asked.

"难道你住的地方不是隔墙有耳吗？"熊说，仿佛感到很惊讶。

"我听说过，但从来没有见过。"她回答。

在洞穴的后部是叮当作响的瀑布，瀑布倾泻到下方池中，发出的声音非常像音乐。和水池相邻的是一块稍微高于地面的厚石板。

"Don't walls have ears where you live?" returned the Bear, as if surprised.

"I've heard they do," she answered, "but I've never seen any before."

At the back of the cave was a little, tinkling waterfall, that splashed into a pool beneath with a sound that was very like music. Near this was a square slab of rock, a little raised above the level of the floor.

跳舞熊开始才艺展示

The Dancing Bear Displays His Talents

66

"请稍坐，亲爱的。我会尽我所能让你开心的，同时也会证明我会跳舞。"熊说。

于是，熊伴着瀑布的音乐开始跳起了舞。他爬上那块平坦的石头上，向着唐可儿优雅地鞠了一躬，然后让自己用一只脚保持平衡，然后是另外一只脚，并且慢慢摇摆转了一个圈，最后恢复原状。

"你觉得怎么样？"他问。

"Kindly take a seat, my dear," said the bear, "and I'll try to amuse you, and at the same time prove that I can dance."

So to the music of the waterfall the bear began dancing. He climbed upon the flat stone, made a graceful bow to Twinkle, and then balanced himself first upon one foot and then upon the other, and swung slowly around in a circle, and then back again.

"How do you like it?" he asked.

"我不太喜欢，我相信我可以做得更好。"唐可儿说。

"可是你不是熊，"他回答。"女孩应该比熊跳得好，你知道的。但并不是每一头熊都能跳舞。如果我有一架手风琴来演奏，而不是伴着这瀑布声，我可能会表演得更好。"

"那我真希望你有一架手风琴。"姑娘说。

"I don't care much for it," said Twinkle. "I believe I could do better myself."

"But you are not a bear," he answered. "Girls ought to dance better than bears, you know. But not every bear can dance. If I had a hand-organ to make the music, instead of this waterfall, I might do better."

"Then I wish you had one," said the girl.

熊又开始跳了，这次他动得更快些，用一种非常滑稽的方式拖着他的双脚。他急着想要证明自己会跳舞，有一两次差点儿从石板上掉下来。有一次他让自己的脚给绊倒了，这逗得唐可儿哈哈大笑。

　　正在他即将结束他的舞蹈的时候，一个陌生的声音喊道：

The Bear began dancing again, and this time he moved more rapidly and shuffled his feet in quite a funny manner. He almost fell off the slab once or twice, so anxious was he to prove he could dance. And once he tripped over his own foot, which made Twinkle laugh.

Just as he was finishing his dance a strange voice cried out:

绿猴子在搞恶作剧
The Green Monkey Makes Mischief

"是熊啊！"一只绿色的猴子跳进洞里，朝着演员扔了一块大石头。石头把熊打下了石板，跌进了瀑布下面的池水中，当他爬出来的时候全身湿透了。

跳舞熊咆哮了一声，以最快的速度向猴子追去，最后追着猴子出了山洞。

"For bear!" and a green monkey sprang into the cave and threw a big rock at the performer. It knocked the bear off the slab, and he fell into the pool of water at the foot of the waterfall, and was dripping wet when he scrambled out again.

The Dancing Bear gave a big growl and ran as fast as he could after the monkey, finally chasing him out of the cave.

唐可儿提起装满了浆果的桶紧随其后，当她再次在山边钻进阳光里的时候，她看到猴子和熊紧紧抱在一起，从他们的咆哮和叽叽喳喳的交谈来看，他们并不是在向对方示好，而是对对方很生气。

　　"你还会向我扔石头的，是吧？"熊喊道。

Twinkle picked up her pail of berries and followed, and when she got into the sunshine again on the side of the hill she saw the monkey and the bear hugging each other tight, and growling and chattering in a way that showed they were angry with each other and not on pleasant terms.

"You *will* throw rocks at me, will you?" shouted the Bear.

"如果我还有机会，我会的。"猴子回答。
"那一下打得很准，很漂亮吧？难道你不是一
个猛子扎进水里的吗？"猴子说着尖声狂笑起来。

　　就在这时，他们一起摔倒了，向着山下
滚去。

　　"松手！"熊大叫。

　　"你放手！"猴子尖叫。

"I will if I get the chance," replied the monkey. "Wasn't that a fine, straight shot? and didn't you go plump into the water, though?" and he shrieked with laughter.

Just then they fell over in a heap, and began rolling down the hill.

"Let go!" yelled the Bear.

"Let go, yourself!" screamed the monkey.

但他们都没有放手，于是他们向着山下滚的速度越来越快，唐可儿最后看到他们身影的时候，他们正从大峡谷底部的灌木丛中弹起来。

But neither of them did let go, so they rolled faster and faster down the hill, and the last that Twinkle saw of them they were bounding among the bushes at the very bottom of the big gulch.

第六章
Chapter VI

灵灵王子
Prince Nimble

"我的天哪！"小姑娘说着向四周看了看，"我差不多在这个陌生的地方迷路了，我不知道往哪个方向走才能回家。"

于是，她坐在草地上，试图想起她从哪条路来的，她应该从哪条路返回才能穿过峡谷返回农场。

"如果滚石在这里的话，他会告诉我的。但是，我现在是独自一人了。"她大声说。

"GOOD gracious!" said the little girl, looking around her; "I'm as good as lost in this strange place, and I don't know in what direction to go to get home again."

So she sat down on the grass and tried to think which way she had come, and which way she ought to return in order to get across the gulch to the farm-house.

"If the Rolling Stone was here, he might tell me," she said aloud. "But I'm all alone."

"哦，不，你不是一个人。"一个细微甜美的声音传来。"我在这里，我知道的事情远比滚石知道的多多了。"

唐可儿仔细地看看这儿，瞅瞅那儿，想要看看刚刚谁在说话，最后，她发现了一只漂亮的蚂蚱栖息在附近的一片草叶上。

"我刚听到说话的是你吗？"她问。

"Oh, no, you're not," piped a small, sweet voice. "I'm here, and I know much more than the Rolling Stone does."

Twinkle looked this way and then that, very carefully, in order to see who had spoken, and at last she discovered a pretty grasshopper perched upon a long blade of grass nearby.

"Did I hear you speak?" she inquired.

唐可儿遇到了灵灵王子

Twinkle Meets Prince Nimble

79

"是啊，我是灵灵王子，是跳跃村最会跳的村民。"蚂蚱回答。

"跳跃村在哪里啊？"唐可儿问。

"哎哟！跳跃村在沟底附近，在你看的那片茂密的草丛中。在你回家的路上，所以我很高兴带你去参观一下。"

"Yes," replied the grasshopper. "I'm Prince Nimble, the hoppiest hopper in Hoptown."

"Where is that?" asked the child.

"Why, Hoptown is near the bottom of the gulch, in that thick patch of grass you see yonder. It's on your way home, so I'd be pleased to have you visit it."

"我不会踩到你吧?" 她问。

"如果你小心点儿是不会踩到我的。蚂蚱不会轻易被踩到的。你知道的,我们很机灵。"灵灵王子回答道。

"好吧,我很乐意去看看一个住着蚂蚱的村子。"唐可儿说。

"Won't I step on some of you?" she asked.

"Not if you are careful," replied Prince Nimble. "Grasshoppers don't often get stepped on. We're pretty active, you know."

"All right," said Twinkle. "I'd like to see a grasshopper village."

"那好，跟着我吧，我会给你带路的。"
灵灵王子说着从草叶上一跃而下，跳在了六英尺开外。

唐可儿站起身跟了上去，眼睛睁得大大的，紧盯着这位灵巧的王子，他跳跃的速度很快，唐可儿为了跟上他不得不一路小跑。灵灵王子会在某一丛草地上或哪块石头上等她，直到唐可儿跟过来才再次前行。

"Then follow me, and I'll guide you," said Nimble, and at once he leaped from the blade of grass and landed at least six feet away.

Twinkle got up and followed, keeping her eye on the pretty Prince, who leaped so fast that she had to trot to keep up with him. Nimble would wait on some clump of grass or bit of rock until the girl came up, and then away he'd go again.

"那儿有多远啊？"唐可儿有一次问他。

"大约 1.5 英里。我们很快就会到那里了，你可以走一英里，我可以走半英里。"他回答道。

"你是怎么知道的呢？"唐可儿问。

"How far is it?" Twinkle once asked him.

"About a mile and a half," was the answer; "we'll soon be there, for you are as good as a mile, and I'm good for the half-mile."

"How do you figure that out?" asked Twinkle.

"哎哟，我总是听说'一个小姐相当于一英里'（'一个小姐相当于一英里'是蚂蚱对谚语的错误理解，谚语原意为'失之毫厘，谬以千里'），而你是个小姐，不是吗？"

"还不是呢，我只是一个小女孩，但如果我不回家吃晚饭，爸爸一定会想我的。"她回答。

"Why, I've always heard that a miss is as good as a mile, and you're a miss, are you not?"

"Not yet," she answered; "I'm only a little girl. But papa will be sure to miss me if I don't get home to supper."

蚂蚱们的舞会
The Grasshoppers' Hop

现在唐可儿开始担心自己赶不上回家吃晚饭了，太阳开始西沉，隐入了辽阔的草原，只洒下一片金色的光芒。小姑娘看见她头顶上方悬浮着最瑰丽的宫殿和城堡。这些宏伟壮观的建筑的尖顶上彩旗飘飘，白银做窗，黄金砌顶。

"那是什么城市啊?" 唐可儿问，静静地站在原地，愣住了。

TWINKLE now began to fear she wouldn't get home to supper, for the sun started to sink into the big prairie, and in the golden glow it left behind, the girl beheld most beautiful palaces and castles suspended in the air just above the hollow in which she stood. Splendid banners floated from the peaks and spires of these magnificent buildings, and all the windows seemed of silver and all the roofs of gold.

"What city is that?" she asked, standing still, in amazement.

空中楼阁

The Castles in the Air

"那不是什么城市。"蚂蚱回答。"只是空中楼阁罢了，可望而不可即。走吧，我的小朋友。我们快到跳跃村了。"

于是唐可儿继续往前走，不久灵灵王子暂停在了一束蜀葵的茎上说：

"现在，小心地在你站的地方坐下来，你就能看到我们的成员了，这是我们召开定期舞会的夜晚，如果你仔细听，你能听到乐队在演奏。"

"That isn't any city," replied the grasshopper. "They are only Castles in the Air—very pretty to look at, but out of everybody's reach. Come along, my little friend; we're almost at Hoptown."

So Twinkle walked on, and before long Prince Nimble paused on the stem of a hollyhock and said:

"Now, sit down carefully, right where you are, and you will be able to watch my people. It is the night of our regular hop—if you listen you can hear the orchestra tuning up."

唐可儿依照灵灵王子的吩咐坐了下来，支着耳朵努力地听，但只听到很低的呼呼声，像是甲虫扇动翅膀的声音。

　　"这是鼓手，他很聪明，确实如此。"灵灵王子说。

　　"天哪！已经是晚上了。"唐可儿吃了一惊。"我这个时候应该在家里，已经上床了！"

She sat down, as he bade her, and tried to listen, but only heard a low whirr and rattle like the noise of a beetle's wings.

"That's the drummer," said Prince Nimble. "He is very clever, indeed."

"Good gracious! It's night," said Twinkle, with a start. "I ought to be at home and in bed this very minute!"

"没关系。"蚂蚱说。"你睡觉在任何时候都可以，但是我们的舞会可是一年一次哟！能亲眼见上一次也算是一个莫大的荣幸吧。"

　　突然，他们周围草地变得灯火通明，那光仿佛来自上千只微小的电灯。唐可儿仔细看了看，发现有数不清的萤火虫在他们周围围成了一个圈，为舞会的场地照明。

"Never mind," said the grasshopper; "you can sleep any time, but this is our annual ball, and it's a great privilege to witness it."

Suddenly the grass all around them became brilliantly lighted, as if from a thousand tiny electric lamps. Twinkle looked closely, and saw that a vast number of fireflies had formed a circle around them, and were illuminating the scene of the ball.

在圈子的中间聚集了数百只大大小小的蚂蚱。个头小点儿的是淡绿色的，中等大小的颜色更绿些，而最大的那些是黄褐色的。

　　但是，最吸引唐可儿的要数乐团的成员了。他们坐在一株大毒菌宽广的顶部的一侧，音乐家们全部是甲虫和大黑虫。

In the center of the circle were assembled hundreds of grasshoppers, of all sizes. The small ones were of a delicate green color, and the middle-sized ones of a deeper green, while the biggest ones were a yellowish brown.

But the members of the orchestra interested Twinkle more than anything else. They were seated upon the broad top of a big toadstool at one side, and the musicians were all beetles and big-bugs.

一只胖胖的水甲虫拉低音大提琴，那琴的大小都快和他自己差不多了，两只漂亮的瓢虫拉小提琴。一只红黑相间颜色鲜艳的金龟子吹长号，砂岩甲虫用翅膀发出像敲鼓的声音。还有一只鞘翅目甲虫，奏出尖锐的声音，像是在吹笛子——当然，唐可儿不知道这些甲虫的名字，她认为他们都只是"虫子"。

A fat water-beetle played a bass fiddle as big and fat as himself, and two pretty ladybugs played the violins. A scarab, brightly colored with scarlet and black, tooted upon a long horn, and a sand-beetle made the sound of a drum with its wings. Then there was a coleopto, making shrill sounds like a flute—only of course Twinkle didn't know the names of these beetles, and thought they were all just "bugs".

虫虫乐队
The Bugs' Orchestra

当乐队开始演奏时，音乐比你想象的更加悦耳。反正，蚂蚱们喜欢，他们已经迫不及待地开始跳舞了。

蚂蚱们的滑稽动作逗得唐可儿一次次大笑，因为他们跳舞的方式是围成一个圈跳，互相跃过对方，然后一位蚂蚱女士和一位蚂蚱男士手牵手后腿直立，让自己的舞伴旋转，直到这个女孩子头晕眼花，只能愣愣地看着他们。

When the orchestra began to play, the music was more pleasing than you might suppose; anyway, the grasshoppers liked it, for they commenced at once to dance.

The antics of the grasshoppers made Twinkle laugh more than once, for the way they danced was to hop around in a circle, and jump over each other, and then a lady grasshopper and a gentleman grasshopper would take hold of hands and stand on their long rear legs and swing partners until it made the girl dizzy just to watch them.

有时候，两只蚂蚱突然跃起来，在空中互相碰撞，然后翻滚着落在地上，那里的其他舞者会绊倒他们。唐可儿看见灵灵王子和其他舞者一起跳着。他的舞伴是一只可爱的绿色蚂蚱，有着一双亮晶晶的黑眼睛和一对天鹅绒似的翅膀。他们没有像其他的蚂蚱那样跌跌绊绊，唐可儿觉得他们的舞跳得确实很优雅。

Sometimes two of them would leap at once, and knock against each other in the air, and then go tumbling to the ground, where the other dancers tripped over them. She saw Prince Nimble dancing away with the others, and his partner was a lovely green grasshopper with sparkling black eyes and wings that were like velvet. They didn't bump into as many of the others as some did, and Twinkle thought they danced very gracefully indeed.

而现在，就在欢乐的气氛达到了高潮的时候，蚂蚱服务员端上了茶点，看上去像覆盖着厚厚糖蜜的草籽，一只大猫突然跳进了圈子。

　　一刹那，所有的灯都灭了，因为萤火虫正四散逃跑，但在黑暗中唐可儿觉得她还能听见低音大提琴声和瓢虫的长笛般的颤音。

And now, while the merriment was at its height, and waiter-grasshoppers were passing around refreshments that looked like grass seeds covered with thick molasses, a big cat suddenly jumped into the circle.

At once all the lights went out, for the fireflies fled in every direction; but in the darkness Twinkle thought she could still hear the drone of the big bass fiddle and the flute-like trill of the ladybugs.

梦中醒来

The Awakening

接下来唐可儿只觉得，有人在摇晃她的肩膀。

"醒醒吧，亲爱的。"是她妈妈说话的声音。"快到晚饭时间了，爸爸正等着你呢，我看你没有捡到一颗蓝莓哦。"

"哎，我捡了呀，好吧。"唐可儿回答道。她坐了起来，先揉了揉眼睛，然后郁闷地看了看她的空锡皮桶。"几分钟前还在桶里呢，真不知道到底发生了什么！"

The next thing Twinkle knew, some one was shaking her shoulder.

"Wake up, dear," said her mother's voice. "It's nearly supper-time, and papa's waiting for you. And I see you haven't picked a single blueberry."

"Why, I picked 'em, all right," replied Twinkle, sitting up and first rubbing her eyes and then looking gravely at her empty tin pail. "They were all in the pail a few minutes ago. I wonder whatever became of them!"

唐可儿奇遇记

出品人：宇 清
策　　划：李 卉
责任编辑：李芬芳　李 卉
装帧设计：Guangfu Design / 张 晖
音乐合成：侯英珊